GW00598675

# SUNSHINE

# THROUGH

# THE

# RAIN

## Bethan Llewellyn-Lloyd

ISBN: 1-905768-07-9
ISBN: 978-1-905768-07-03

Printed by Aspect Design, Malvern
Tel: 01684 561567

# CONTENTS

# PHOTOGRAPHS
## by Alison Willis

# NATURE

**Let me stop and know Your creation**
The warm breeze caresses me
Calms my emotion.
In the wind You touch me
The spirit blows round me.

Let me look at Your creation
The rolling hills
The majesty of the trees
Their leaves rustling in the breeze
The wind of the spirit circling me.

Let me listen to Your creation
As You speak to me
Words carried on the breeze
Enter me in Your stillness
Tune in to Your melody.

Lord I come to meet You here
To seek You, to find You near.
It's easier in tranquillity
Without disturbance -
Hold me that I might hear.

# Lying at my feet

The sky shimmers

And shatters in ripples

Sifting the sand.

Sparkling silver rivers

Ebb and flow

Come and go.

A frothing boom glides over

And strands the glistening bubbles

That flicker, catching the light

Blown by the chill breeze.

Roaring, roaring

Surf soaring

Crashing and splashing

With the turning tide.

Sea smoothed sand

Meets the land.

**Our web of gossamer**
Spins eternally
Droplets
Glistening
In the light.
Shining
Sparkling
Then hidden
Waiting...
Bulging in breezes
Flexing
Stretching
In the draughts
Of living.
Sticky
Clinging
Tenaciously holding
In struggles
Of life.
Lord, cloak me
In Your
Gossamer thread.

## In the stillness

I feel You near.

Amongst the trees and unfurling leaves

I feel You here.

In the sound of birdsong

And dripping rain

I can hear You again and again.

In the joy of a flower

I feel Your power.

The bee's hum

Your song to be sung.

Soft moss and green fronds

In this world You live on.

I know You are near

I feel Your presence here.

## Nature's beauty transforming

Her grandeur

Enrapture.

Sky and sea

Spaciousness.

Craggy rock

And rippling stream

Salt washed pebbles

And delta marked sand

For the sea has retreated

Away from the land.

A stillness pervades

The storm has long gone.

The sea smoothed sand

Wet

Reflects

The sky's pastel hues

Of oranges and blues.

Wispy white clouds

Mirror wisps of water

Whipped off the wave tops

Spreading across the sand

Creeping to the rocks

Washing bubbles over

The rippled sand

Moving the mirrored sky.

The glowing sun

Sets the sea and sand

Alight with fingers of fire

Waves peak

Fold and crash into

The misty blue.

The colours are gentle

Yet filled with a brilliant glow

The air is still

Full of majesty

Where land and sea

Draw together

I come to You.

## Clear mountain streams

Cascade in falls
Down the rock face
Crashing in white turbulence
Sending a fine spray
Circling above.
Incessant sound
Thundering on
Leading into clear
Deep pools
Tranquil and calm.
Still water
Allows the light
To reach the coloured stones
Resting in their cool bed.
Sunlight twinkles on the
Wind-ruffled surface
Depths lost to view.
In your eyes I see
The water flowing
The crashing fall
The rippling stream
The sunlight dancing
In merriment
And deep, still pools.

Your steady gaze
In the knowledge of love.
His love unfathomable
Steady and calm.
Still water casts
A reflection
Clear and crisp.
In your eyes I see
That deep, still pool
Your gaze and His
Mingle in your eyes.
His love shines
Through you to me.
Life ruffles the surface
And the reflection is lost
Shattered
Scattered by the breeze
But the water flows on
It has not dried up
Stillness will return
And the deep, still pool
Of His love in tranquillity
Will show again in your eyes.

## The mysterious expectancy of morning

Sparkles in the bejewelled land
Glistening with dewdrops
Reflecting a brilliance
That awoke with the rosy dawn.
In the calm stillness
For a moment life waits to waken.
The sweet cool air
Laden with a frisson
Of awaiting opportunity.
The haze over the lowland
Seeps away
The mountain reaches upward
Into the depths above
As changing colours creep
Over its craggy crown.
Nature is stirring
But let man sleep awhile
His interference must wait
And keep the spell unbroken
By his intrusive sounds.
Let the wheeling oystercatcher
Rule the rippling river mouth
Governed by the paling moon
That draws the tides
In the ever changing beauty of the estuary.
This moment can only last in a daydream.
For now the moment has gone

Changed by the rising sun
The turning tide
And the rising wind.
But treasure it in the mind's eye
To gaze again and know its beauty.

The wind stirs the water
In white topped ripples
Tearing away summer's tranquillity
Searing through the leafless oaks
Clinging to the rocky outcrops
Tight buds waiting in the cold.
A grey shroud has wrapped the scene
In a cold damp blanket of winter.
All has closed in as the beating rain
Slants over the sheltering sheep beneath the hill.
The mountain lost in cloud
Stands heavily with its cold gloomy shadow
Sinking into life around
Seeping into the spirit
Chill and lowering.
Land and man too cowering
Beneath the cold might of winter.
Draw near to the fire's warming comfort
And dream of that dew laden day
Of sunrise in summer
Trusting in its coming.

## I smell with joy

The perfume of flowers.

Red roses' scent

Fills my head

With lovely notions

A romantic potion.

Honeysuckle sweet

Fills my nostrils

With aroma.

Memories of youth

Expectant.

The sun shining

On flowers and on my skin

Brings a warmth to my heart

No other heat can bring.

## Surging sea

Scurries

Sending saline

Ripples

Swiftly smoothing

Submerging sand.

Sunlight

Sparkling

Dazzling

Twinkling.

Surf

Crashing

And surging

Rhythmically

Roaring.

# SEARCHING

## Freedom to do as we please?

Freedom to follow or not,

Freedom to use or abuse,

To be unfettered, unchained.

Freedom to hurt, be unkind.

Free to turn against anything, anyone.

But freedom needs discipline

Or freedom can no longer

Be free.

For total freedom

Could be taking a liberty.

A freedom to be bound

To Your set of rules

Leaves us free

From an evil tyranny.

Never totally free

For everyone has a responsibility

To all surrounding them.

In You is the guide to freedom,

An opportunity for liberty,

A discipleship of discipline

To be free.

# Time is given

And time is taken away.

Time flown by

Was yesteryear, yesterday.

Time is coming,

A time is stretching ahead.

Time is for living

Alive, now, in living bread.

The past is gone

But has shaped the way.

The past is breaking

Into a new day.

The future out there

Is unknown and exciting.

For fortune You bring

In Your love through our living.

## There is something I have to do for You

But what, where, when and why

I do not know.

I feel Your presence creep within

Release a sigh at sensing You.

My voice prattles on within my head

But now be still to hear You instead.

Pause interminable restless thoughts

Driving at life in never-ending activity.

Be still

Retreat to the rhythm of my breath

Gentle rising and falling of my chest.

Let care flow out and the spirit flow in.

# I look for the light

The light of the world

The guiding light

More precious than gold.

That heavenly light

Which can shine in me

To lighten my load

And show God's word.

It mustn't be hidden

But allowed to glow

For God's purpose

Which as yet I don't know.

Allow my light to be friendly

Welcoming

Inviting others in

For only You see

How the rays might shine

Through a hard heart's crevice

Warming within

Starting a spark

Of new life and living.

# I'm lost

I'm out of touch
No sensitivity
No creativity.
Communication cut.
Love lost in life.
Cut loose
Untethered, unbound
I'm locked into emptiness
Inwardly dying.
Faltering flame flickering
In the daily draughts
Of living.
Freedom stifled by a tyranny
Gnawing into my being
Keeping me apart from You.
Suppressing what is within
I conceal You.
Longing to openly find You
To invite You in.
Tension rises
In the strengthening light.
I turn aside
Dying in denying.

## Lord, help me see

That I, like the vine

And the living tree

Need You as the gardener

Tending me.


I need Your loving care

I need God

And others to share

In Your word and in prayer.


Water me with living water

Filling my heart

With Your spirit

Prune out all that is evil

That I may bear Your fruit.

# Stand firm in the knowledge of the Lord

Never releasing His grip on you.

Keep holding His hand fast

Trusting in His caring.

We cannot see what His purpose may be

But we know His love.

Sometimes "unjust"

Sometimes "unfair"

We cannot understand

The hard times in our lives.

Why, oh why?

And why me?

Why them?

But keep on holding.

Give Him your fear.

Place yourselves and your cares

Into His hands.

You are so special to Him

As well as to us.

We all keep caring

Continue sharing

In His love.

Lost in the fog of the unknown

Of uncertainty

Place your hand in His

Your trust in Him

And He will take the strain

Caring for you, upholding you

Throughout life's moments of pain.

# *FAITH*

## Bright light shining

Flat on a form

Shapeless.

Shadows give line

A depth of being,

Contouring and lifting.

Life's darker moments

Give shape and recognition

To the joy of the light time

Quickly forgotten.

The contrasts of life

Give depth

More meaning

So find a balance

In the dark times of living.

# Lord, may I reflect

Your light

In my life

For I know

You are here

As Your love makes clear.

Let me be

A mirror for Thee.

What I see in You

Showing in all I do.

Shining out

Without any doubt

Reflecting You.

## Tears filled my eyes

After hearing those words.

Words spoken to all

Yet meant for me.

Oh "conflict within"

And "conflict without"

There's conflict in my heart

Without any doubt.

Tonight in that sermon I realised

As the tears welled up

And pricked my eyes

Its true

Half measures will not do

So Lord I give myself to You.

## The elixir of stillness

Draws me nearer to You.

Light-headed and fearless

Of what You might do.

You speak to me

And take my hand

Filling my being

With Your love

For You understand

The intoxication

Of love in the stillness.

I must wait

Be patient

Be guided by You.

## Truth in virtue

In virtue truth lies.

Hold fast

In virtuousness

Or else truth dies.

Grasp Jesus

Let Him shine in you

His virtue in all you do.

Evil lurks

Will taunt and taint.

Never let it in.

For Jesus' sake don't sin.

He'll hold you

Whate'er you go through.

Invite Him in.

Conviction lies paramount

Live by it

Never doubt

Hold fast.

For in virtue truth lies.

Truth in virtue.

## When You call my name

I want to be listening.
When You call my name
I want to hear.

When You stand by me
I'll look into Your face.
When You stand by me
I'll know Your grace.

When You lift me up
I'll come with You
When You lift me up
My life is for You.

I know You're there
Feel Your love and care.
I know You're there
Take me, I'm ready to share.

## Walking along on level ground

Stepping out is easy.

Striding along in brilliant sun

Under azure sky

My heart and head are high.


The track uneven underfoot

Needs sturdy boots

And a steadier tread

As the ground inclines

The path twisting upwards

Breathing quickens

Eyes downward

Watching where each foot

Should fall.


Rising slowly in the stillness

The mountain calls me.

The body tires with aching limbs

And lack of breath.

I turn and sit.

Spread out below and reaching far

I see Your hand.

A silver ribbon river

Twists to the sparkling sea.

Rising from the tree lined valley

Sheep pasture in patches of green

Is threaded with stone walls

And changes into violet heather

Warm against the grey rocks.

Reward for upward toil

Is spread below.


As I climb life's upward path

You let me stop to turn around

And show me Your wonders

Your riches.

The prize for effort is beauty

Beyond compare.

May the way up my mountain path

However steep and precipitous

Be undertaken with You at my side

In the knowledge

Of joy in Your presence.

## A song of childhood fills the air

"No crib for a bed"

But these are not children

Without any cares.

The melody of innocence spinning its charm

"Laid down his sweet head"

These are grown adults and are

Drowning their cares.

The words are familiar

"Look down where He lay"

But sadly their conduct

Makes their heads sway.

"And fit us for heaven"

Only where are they seeking

For that message today?

## We make it all tinsel and glamour

Presents and jovial clamour

But for You not a sparkle

Except for Your star

For You all the clamour

Was crowds in the street

Humble, no glamour

Amidst hay smelling sweet.

Born into a shelter for oxen and ass

You came down from heaven

To live with us.

## Sadness and sorrow

Tears and despair

As You hang on the cross I know

Deep love and care.

Weary and worn

Lost and forlorn

I stare and stare

Your body has gone.

Grief and bewilderment

Anger and fear

I did not know

You could be so near.

Gently with care

Softly with love

You spoke my name

I found You here.

You are alive and speak to me

You are here and live in me.

You are the risen Lord.

## Thank You, Lord

For Your gift to us.

Thank You, Lord

For forgiving us.

Thank You, Lord

For Your outstretched hand

Pierced for us.

Thank You, Lord

For unending strength

Upholding us.

Thank You, Lord

For saving us.

# RENEWAL

**As soon as I feel I'm getting along just fine**

I stop and realise that I've left You behind.

In worldly terms I'm forging ahead

But in not talking to You I'm inwardly dead.

The satisfaction of getting things done

Evaporates when I know how wrong

I am to keep forgetting You

By not inviting You in to all I do.

## Activity, activity, I'm lost in my activity

Busy, busy, busy, bustle has taken over me.

Clock watching, living by lists

The driving, throbbing pace thrusts on

Unrelenting

Until sleep submerges activity.

There's no time for space....

Put it on the list.

Value it, create it and use it.

Replenish sagging energy

Renewing through the re-entering spirit.

Relax in renewal

In communication

Taking time to listen

To the Lord.

## Be still and rest awhile

Sit quietly and simply be
Let go the minutes carefully watched
And see the grasses grow.
Seedy branches waving
In the passing breeze
Beneath the spreading trees
Lending their shade
From June's searing sun.
Let hurrying drift away
And look at nature's gentle face
Quietly smiling at her own pace.
See the beauty in the buttercup
Its petals glistening, open to the sun.
It knows no hurry
Tracing time by the sun's path.
Just lie and rest awhile
Stare at the sky, know its infinity
Feel the spirit
In loveliness and lack of care.

# Have I lost touch with myself?

No contact with my inner self.

Hiding my inner core from view

An outer layer covering

An impenetrable coating

Not letting true life in

Feeling lost in mundane activity

Emotion submerged by practicality

A well capped.

Unstop the spring

Let the fountain rise up

Bubble to the surface

Overflow, sparkling and gurgling

In joyous living

Flowing through me

Flooding my whole being

Seeping and spreading.

For too long suppressed.

Now let it spurt forth

Allow it to flow

Transforming barrenness into fertility.

I'd lost You Lord

But You well up within.

My tears welcome You in.

## Dense

White

Blank

Engulfing

Surrounding.

Still

Chill

Damp

Ice clinging

Freezing.

I'm numbed

By a cold dampness

Surrounding

Penetrating.

Vision bland.

A freezing fog

Grips my spirit

Freezing it into

Numbness.

Blanks out my vision

To white nothingness.

Lost and cold

I'm not seeing You

Not feeling You

Your warm hand

Lost in the frozen cloud.

Life has gone cold

Without the touch

Of Your spirit.


Rays shining through

Warm fingers reaching

Through the trees

Thawing the crystals.

Beams stretching out

Piercing the blank whiteness

Warming

Brightening

The spirit alightening

Touching within

Reviving

Life giving

Touch me

Enter in.

# *MUSIC*

## Horses grazing in flat fields

Threaded by hedge and ditch

Combines that cut the ripened corn

Moving in their dusty cloud.

Silhouetted against the heat hazed sky

A shape rises up

In command of the level land

Turrets and tower stand solid and grey

Mysterious on the horizon.

A cathedral church waiting for discovery

Its magnificence man's offering to the Maker.


Through huge ancient iron-studded doors

God's house welcomes.

Great pillars reach aloft

To the pictured ceiling high above.

Its grandeur overwhelms.

We are about to be a minute part

Of its great history

As, for a fleeting moment,

The privilege to sing beneath

The octagon tower leads

To affirmation at the communion rail.

Your forgiveness falls from above.

Flowing within, Your love drowns other emotions.

My heart, touched by the Spirit

Longs to be nearer You

Seeks to share with You.

The sound of singing rises

Drifting through the heat-laden air

It resonates round, an ethereal sound in worship.

A gift we have to lend

As sound floats round

Each person a part of the whole

To sing and add to eternity.

## Quiet

Still
The tranquillity I crave surrounds me.
No rush
No bustle
Time fills the air
In the quietness.
No one
To cut the quiet.
No voices near
To penetrate the peace.
No movement
Breaking the moments of magic
Of stillness.
Come close in the quiet
For I know You are near
When the stillness descends
And the Spirit can appear
To enter in
The core of my being.
Such rare moments of silence
I should seek
And create
But life crowds in
Stealing time
Engulfing me.

I drown, suffocated
Asphyxiated by activity.
In opposition of tension and relaxation
One must contrast with the other
The one lending poignancy
In the other's beauty and exhilaration
A counterpoint of movement and rest
Parts in juxtaposition
Enhancing and highlighting
Creating a whole
To seep deep within
Pianissimo in tranquillity
Welcome after
Fortissimo activity.
Artistic awareness moves within
Heightening emotion
Leaving a craving
Yearning the passion
Stirring sensation
Longing... to love.
Stop, stifling living
Let life rise up
And shine as rays
Piercing the mist-laden air.

## Joyous

Brilliant.
Beams of love
Radiating in the dullness
Of monotony.
Let the note change
To rise and fall
To quicken and turn
Into melody
Spun into music's beauty
Spearing depths
Speaking in tongues of sound
Moving internally
Touching
Gently
Touching within
Caressing
Awakening
An awareness
A knowledge
Of Him in me
Of me in Him.

# If music be the food of love

Let me love You Lord through sounds.

Vibrating passion

Stirring hearts

Speaking harmonies

Of the soul.

Echoes of joy

Notes of despair

Sweet songs.

My soul sings to You

My heart cries to You

In rapturous sound

In sadness

In calm and humility.

This gift of music given to me

Let me use it to Your glory.

## In the music

Let our souls take flight

In the touch of sound

I sense your caresses

Notes our communication -

Staccato, legato their many shades

Share sensuality

An anger, a passion.

In calm and tranquillity

In discordant agony

In the unleashing of emotion.

## Something within

Makes me reach up high

Driving inside

Sets my sights at the top.

I can't get that far

Fall short

Goals unattained.

Thoughts reach for perfection

In action

Leave me falling

Frustrated in failure

To achieve the goal in my mind.

Why try to leap?

Be content

In being

Let gentle thoughts invade

Lifting, rising slowly

Imperceptibly

Trust the direction

Without thrusting and frustration

Allow the Lord to direct me.

# *LOVE*

## Love is yellow

Bright, clear and warm

Love is red

With anger and passion

Like a flaming dawn.

Love is green

The spring growth of a beech leaf.


Yellow brings warmth

No longing

Secure.

Red brings an anger

Frustration

Anguish

Yearning.

Green brings new growth

Lush pastures serene.

Green brings the Lord.

Help my love that is green.

## Lord, craving love

Gnaws deep inside

Floods throughout with a passionate sensibility

That brings me alive

Awakens my every nerve to You

Quickens my senses

And drives me onward

Seeking Your spirit

To mould my reawakening

In Your love.

## Do we punish those we love

When things are beyond their control?

Can we justify irrationality

When life is dark,

A black cavernous hole?

Your love for us

Should we turn it to hate

When events aren't as we'd like?

Behaving in the extreme

Does it compensate?

On wings of adversity

Like an eagle we should fly

Rising and gliding

Riding, never stalling

Over the storm.

You support us

Whatever the adversity

If we turn to You

Ask You personally.

How can we turn

The love You give

Into hatred in adversity?

**She brings me flowers**

To make me smile

When I am cross

Or tired and scowl

She brings me flowers to make me smile.

Today in bed

Feeling unwell

Three from her garden

Her gift with a smile.

Marigold and eschscholzia

Glow golden and bold

Bring sunshine and laughter

And echo her smile.

With care and with love

She passes to me

Flowers clasped in her

Dainty hand.

Gratitude and love

Grow in me

Show in her youthful simplicity.

# The mist rises gently

From the sodden earth

Drawn by a glow in the paled sky

Its beauty painful, beguiling

Creating a landscape

Of haziness and gentle hues.

Something leaps forth

From the saddened heart

Inspired by your enlightenment

And the loveliness together

A friendship

Of rare worth and closeness.

A rare richness

In companionship.

Life's melody weaves

Accompanied

Together

Whole.

## What is it I cannot see

But sense?
What is it I cannot touch
But feel?
What is it in you
I long to reach?
What insight do I need
In this tenderness?
What sensibility is it?
What response?
What sympathy?
What understanding
Mixes with the thrill
Of cordiality.
Something profound
Lies hidden
Awaits an awakening
And releasing
An unfreezing
In Spring's thaw
Leaking out
Dissipating
In compassion.

# *BEREAVEMENT*

## Choked with a selfish sadness

At the fear of losing you

I realise the great gladness

Brought by knowing you.

And on we move

Along life's way

Acknowledging the touch

Of His love through another.

In gratitude

In the teaching of others

The touching of lives

Showing His way.

In sadness I seek solitude

To retreat from life momentarily

To recompose

That God may restore

An equilibrium

In new opportunity

Another open door

A new sign along life's way

In thanks for the gifts of the past

And trust in His bounty ahead.

# A robin trills his merry tune

A herald to all continuing.

Nature is renewing.

Shafts of light

Twinkle in his beady eye

Looking quizzically at me

Head to one side and cheerfully

He hops across the earth

In serenity.

For here You are

In the tranquil garden

Renewing and enriching

By Your beauty.

She knew this scene too

The dug earth

The humble snowdrop

A messenger of coming spring.

She enjoyed the robin's beady twinkling eye

Its company as gardener's friend.

Here we stand to respect the end

Of an important era

Remembering, cherishing and continuing

What you gave us

In our lives.

## The web of life so delicately spun

With a fine gossamer thread easily undone.

Its only strength lies in life's equilibrium

In a balance undisturbed,

So easily broken.

The life of the world should be held

Within Your hands to show the way

For man is too meddlesome

And will cause its decay.

How much do we care

For another man's plight?

How many must bear pain

Suffering for our delight?

The North, the South

Must express their views

Can they find a solution

To a world of pollution?

A world of poverty

Only some of riches

A world of indulgence

Of selfish leeches.

# For a moment you look in

At a life removed

From your reality.

From warmth and comfort

You gaze at us....

Starving, staring masses

Shivering in the freezing

Hillsides.

Huddling under plastic

Lying on earth to rest

In our forgotten land of starkness.

Christmas surrounds you

A rosy glow of fairy lights

A flickering fire

Tinsel and baubles sparkling

Sending out a joyous message.

Here

We barely survive in the cold

Starving

Shivering

Dying.

## A hillside a home?

Sky a roof?

Earth a floor?

Biting winds

No walls.

Crouching

Huddling

Vacant staring

Moaning

Crying

Sorrow and dying.

Starving babies

Cradled in bony arms

Breasts hanging

No suckling.

Lying

Helpless

Sick

No-one caring.

War

Politics

Refugees suffering.

## Eyes widened

Stare out

From a body

Shivering

In the icy cold.

The muddied earth

Turned white

And frozen

By the falling snow.

First it was rain

Pouring down

Making a quagmire

Drenching us to the skin

Our only clothes

Sodden.

No heat to dry us.

Now it's so cold

Shivering children

Stare at their life's bleakness

Numbed and dying.

### Remember

It takes time.

Living takes time.

Nothing is instant.

You can't fight it,

Time,

But go with it

Fill it to the brim

Gently pouring

It full of life's riches

Allowing it to be

Used to the full.

Never spill a drop

For time wasted will never return.

Place what you have

On the scales of living

And balance time

With the energy you're given

And use them together

For the fullness

Of living.